abcs
of
Gardening

Dylanna Press

Editor: Julie Grady

A is for Annuals

Annual plants are like magical creatures! They come to life each spring, bringing bursts of color and beautiful blooms all summer long. They can be grown from tiny seeds or purchased as small seedlings ready for planting. Annuals don't last forever, but the joy they bring is worth it!

B is for Bees

Bees are hardworking helpers in the garden! Each bee has an important job to do, from collecting nectar and pollen to feeding their hive. Without bees, our gardens would be missing out on many colorful blooms and delicious fruits. They help keep garden plants healthy and gorgeous, so we can enjoy all that nature has to offer!

C is for Compost

Composting is like a little miracle for the garden! It's an easy way to recycle kitchen scraps and yard clippings into something wonderful. It creates nutrient-rich soil that helps our plants grow bigger and healthier. Plus, it helps reduce waste, so we can all do our part to keep Earth beautiful!

D is for Daffodils

Daffodils are like little yellow suns! These cheerful flowers bring a burst of color and life to the garden. They have bright, trumpet-shaped blooms that look like they're smiling up at us. When you see daffodils in bloom, it's a reminder that spring is coming and warmer days are ahead!

E is for Earthworms

Earthworms are like the garden's secret superheroes! They help to keep our soil healthy by digging tunnels and aerating it. This makes it easier for plants to get their nutrients, so they can grow nice and strong. Earthworms also help break down decaying material into compost that helps feed the growing plants.

F is for Fertilizer

Fertilizer is like vitamins for plants! It helps them to stay strong and healthy by providing them with essential nutrients that they need to grow. Adding fertilizer to your garden is like having a special secret ingredient in your recipes – it'll make everything just right!

ECO
fertilizer

50 kg

G is for Greenhouse

Greenhouses are like little indoor gardens! They help to keep plants warm and safe from the elements outside, while still getting all the sunlight and water they need. Greenhouses can produce wonderful fruits, vegetables, flowers, and even herbs that we would not be able to grow without them.

H is for Herbs

Growing herbs in the garden is like having your very own mini-supermarket! Herbs are like little magical plants that fill your garden with wonderful scents and flavors. Plus, they can be used to cook delicious meals, create calming teas, and add a special touch of color and texture to your outdoor space.

I is for Insects

Insects in the garden have important jobs to do! They help pollinate flowers and crops, providing us with food. They also eat other insects, helping to keep our gardens free from pests, and they are an important part of the food chain.

J  is for Jam

Did you know you can make your own tasty jam from the sweet and juicy fruits grown in your garden? Making jam is a fun activity that can be enjoyed by all ages, and with the right ingredients, you'll be able to enjoy the flavor of summer all year round! Let's see what kind of yummy creation we can make!

K is for Kale

Kale is a super healthy and tasty vegetable that's perfect for growing in your garden! It's loaded with important vitamins and minerals to keep you healthy. Plus, it tastes great in salads, smoothies and other recipes. Plant some kale seeds, watch them grow, and see the leaves change from light green to deep green as they mature.

L is for Ladybugs

Did you know that ladybugs are nature's pest control super-stars? That's right, these little bugs love to eat pesky garden pests like aphids, mites, and other insects that can harm your plants. In fact, just one ladybug can eat up to 50 aphids in a single day - that's a lot of bug-busting power!

M  is for Mulch

Mulch is like a cozy blanket for your plants! It's a layer of material that you put on top of the soil to help protect your plants from the sun, retain moisture, and keep weeds from growing. There are lots of different kinds of mulch like wood chips, straw, and shredded leaves - each type adds its own texture and color.

N is for Native Plants

Native plants are the types of plants that grow naturally in your area. These plants have learned to grow and thrive on their own and they know all the secrets of the environment. By planting native plants in your garden, you can help create a special habitat that provides food and shelter for beneficial insects and animals.

O is for Organic

An organic garden is a special type of garden where you don't use any harmful chemicals or pesticides. When you use methods like composting, natural fertilizers, and beneficial insects your plants thrive while being gentle to the environment. A beautiful organic garden keeps both you and the planet happy and healthy!

P is for Pruning

Pruning in the garden is like giving your plants a much-needed haircut! Just like you get a trim to keep your hair looking nice, pruning helps plants stay healthy and looking their best. Pruning removes dead or damaged branches and stems, which helps promote new growth and encourages the plant's natural shape.

Q is for Quality Soil

Quality soil is the foundation of a good garden! It's the special dirt that you put in your garden to give your plants all the nutrients they need to grow healthy roots, leaves, and flowers. And just like how we need healthy food to grow, plants need healthy soil to grow too!

GARDEN SOIL

R is for Roots

Plant roots are the hidden part of the plant that lives underground. They anchor plants in place and help them stay healthy and strong! But roots are not just good for holding the plant in the ground – they're also like little straws that suck up water and nutrients from the soil.

Parts Of Root

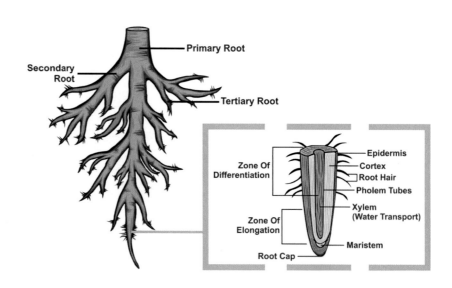

Primary Root

Secondary Root

Tertiary Root

Zone Of Differentiation

Zone Of Elongation

Root Cap

Epidermis

Cortex

Root Hair

Pholem Tubes

Xylem (Water Transport)

Maristem

is for Seeds

Seeds come in many types of shapes and sizes, and each one has the power to create a unique plant. They might look small and unassuming, but inside each one is a future plant bursting with potential. You can plant seeds in your garden by digging a small hole in the soil and dropping the seed inside. Then you can cover it with soil and water it gently. And just like that, you've started your very own plant from a tiny seed!

VEGETABLE SEEDS

tomato   pepper   cabbage   carrot   beet

T is for Tools

Tools help you take care of your garden. From watering cans to trowels, each tool has its own use to make gardening easier and more fun. You can use a shovel to dig holes, a rake to collect leaves, and a hoe to break up soil. With the right tools, you can help your garden grow big and strong.

U is for Urban Garden

Urban gardens are like secret oases in the middle of the city! They are special gardens that people create in small spaces like balconies, rooftops, or even on the sidewalk. Urban gardens are a great way to grow your own food, connect with nature, and make your city a more beautiful place.

V  is for vegetables

Veggies are superfoods that provide your body with vital vitamins and minerals that help keep you healthy and strong. Plus, they're fun to eat – whether you fry them up, roast them in the oven, or even munch on them raw. There are all kinds of cool veggies to grow in the garden like carrots, tomatoes, and even purple cauliflower!

W is for weeds

Weeds are like sneaky little villains in the garden! They're the plants that try to steal all the sunshine, water, and nutrients from your favorite flowers and veggies. But don't worry - you can be a superhero and defeat those pesky weeds! All you have to do is put on your gardening gloves and pull them out of the ground.

X  is for xeriscaping

Xeriscaping is an eco-friendly way of gardening that helps you use less water and still have a beautiful garden. You can do this by planting special plants that don't need a lot of water, using mulch to keep the soil moist, and using rocks and stones to create a desert landscape.

Y

is for Yard

Your yard is the perfect place for fun and adventure! It's a place where you can run around, let your imagination run wild, and make all sorts of discoveries. Whether it's finding a secret hiding spot behind a tree or uncovering a forgotten patch of wildflowers, your yard is a place for discovering nature and having adventures.

Z is for zucchini

Zucchini are a garden favorite! They're the perfect crop to grow, since they produce big results with little effort. With just one zucchini plant, you can expect lots of zucchinis throughout the summer and fall. But the best part? There are so many fun ways to prepare and enjoy your zucchini bounty – from fried zucchini to zucchini bread to zoodles!

Made in the USA
Las Vegas, NV
14 March 2024

87169837R00019